Finance Tips & Tricks for Young Adults

ENGLISH EDITION

VOLUME 1

First published in 2022

Copyright © Daniel Donnelly

Sherwood Finance Limited
4/129 Kensington High Street
London W8 6BD England

The moral rights of the authors have been asserted.

ISBN: 9780645403510 (pbk)

The right of Daniel Donnelly to be identified as the authors of this work has been asserted by them in accordance with the *Copyright Amendment (Moral Rights) Act 2000*.

All rights reserved. Except as permitted under the Australian *Copyright Act 1968*, no part of this publication may be reproduced, stored in a retrieval system, or transmitted in any form or by any means, electronic, mechanical, photocopying, recording or otherwise without prior written permission from the author.

Contents

Topic 1:	History	3
Topic 2:	Trading	6
Topic 3:	Budgeting	8
Topic 5:	Working	16
Topic 6:	Income	22
Topic 7:	Savings	28
Topic 8:	Taxes	40
Topic 8:	Insurance	43
Topic 9:	Borrowing	47
Topic 10:	Credit reporting	64
Conclusion		69
Glossary		72

Introduction

Let's start with the story of Robin Hood, way back in the 14th century. Robin was born in Sherwood Forest, England, where he gained a reputation for being an excellent soldier. Throughout the years, his story has lived on, though it has deviated somewhat since. Our team here at Sherwood Finance wants to hold onto the lessons that Robin Hood taught us and bring them back into the modern world. We hope his great deeds inspire you and that you can learn from his mistakes. Known for being outgoing and adventurous, Robin Hood had a firm grasp on the goings-on in and around Sherwood Forest. In addition, he became famous for being a friend to the poor and a believer in justice and equality for people from all walks of life. His story and values have helped shape our feelings about ethics. However, far from a story about a mythical character, this book discusses a number of useful financial products and the risks involved when using them, information on how to apply for a mortgage, and so much more. Enjoy!

Topic 1: History

A long time ago, before money existed, life was much simpler. People could take care of themselves and their families, hunt for the food they needed, and travel from one place to another, whenever necessary. Money wasn't a factor. Back then, people learned new skills and specialised in different things, which, in turn, improved and increased the productivity, quantity and quality of services and goods, and led to more than was necessary.

Since money, as we know it, was yet to be invented, bartering was used when items were exchanged. We can see examples of this in modern life; anyone who specialises in a trade often gives a service or goods for something in return—from farmers to blacksmiths.

Over time, bartering became less common, and as the trading evolved, humans used precious metals as payment instead. For example, gold could be moulded and rare, so it became accepted as a trading commodity. Weight was often the key factor in deciding the value and was a significant step towards the way we use money today.

Using gold in trading was revolutionary, but it wasn't a perfect system. For example, if you consider when a large payment is required for buying a property, it wasn't workable for the buyer to carry so much. However, a solution was reached when bankers and goldsmiths began holding payments to make it easier for people on both ends (buyers and sellers) to make their transactions.

Gold is no longer used as physical currency today; the coins and cash we use now, made from far less precious materials, aren't worth much. However, a coin's material doesn't detract from the financial worth of our currencies; rather, governments guarantee the value of a currency, which allows swift transactions. This guarantee is a stable method of payment that can be valuable, even if the physical or digital money itself isn't made of gold or precious materials.

Financial transactions began with issued notes, which stated how much gold was owned. Most people used paper notes to make transactions in the marketplace since actual gold determined a note's value, allowing people to accept the issued notes as payment for their goods. These notes became the paper bills that are used today. Then coins were made with cheaper metals such as copper, while still representing the same value.

A long time ago, bartering was the most common trading method for quite a while, even though the issues came along with it. The system worked fine when two people agreed on a trade, but sometimes individuals weren't in agreement. A farmer, for example, might consider their stock to be worth more than what someone is offering. There is, of course, trading for something else, but again, they both need to agree that their trade was of equal value. When a farmer can't find anything they believe to be worth trading, an issue arises. If they find nothing they feel is a fair transaction, they might disagree. It's easy to see why bartering wouldn't work as well for everyday use nowadays.

People need money to survive. Most transactions worldwide are electronic, using visa cards or even QR codes to complete the transactions. And over the last ten to twenty years, we have seen a decrease in paper money in favour of electronic payments. For example, we receive our income electronically and pay most of our bills. To generate the income required to pay the bills, get supplies or buy gifts for friends or family, we head out to work to earn a salary. So, here are just a couple of examples of different sources of income, and as you start out in the workforce, you will become an employee.

Topic 2: Trading

The world that Robin Hood lived in differs from the one we know today. Back in the 14th century in England, transactions were completed through simpler methods, such as bartering or trading. For example, farmers could trade their produce for hand-forged tools from a blacksmith. While professions are still important today, making transactions for services and goods is much more complicated. In the modern world, we make transactions whenever we want, which makes it very difficult to trade goods and services in return for desired items/skills; hence, having a separate commodity representing value is crucial in our fast-paced world, allowing people to accept payments for goods and services. Because of this, the medium of exchange and having a monetary system are essential and more suitable for today's world than a barter system.

The asset is a value (and that value is stored for later use). Money that you earn can be saved, divided and used for different transactions, thus making it a versatile commodity. Our money system needs to keep its value, which is one of the main reasons why inflation, which can affect the value of money, can cause a problem. Money is not only in the form of paper bills, since the money you

Topic 2: Trading

hold in accounts, deposits, and even investments can also be utilised. The financial services industry wouldn't exist if people didn't need help to spend it, and to save it. There are many professionals offering such services to anyone with valuable assets.

Topic 3: Budgeting

Did you know that the word we use for budget today derives from the word *bougette*, meaning *purse* in Old French.

A budget is a plan set to decide the amount of money you aim to receive and pay out over the time. This could be a week, month, year, or any other amount of time. The primary goal of budgeting is to think ahead, allowing you to understand how much you'll have left to spend or save after all the necessities have been catered to.

A budget can involve looking at your bills and living expenses and using them to decide how much you're spending on average. This includes all outgoings to help you better understand how much money is required for travel expenses, food, and various other daily payments that you make.

Those with an irregular income are likely to find budgeting even more crucial since it requires people to be more considerate of their bills and expenses and if they will be due before you receive your next payment.

Keeping track of your finances

Keeping track of your finances is vital, and doing so will require regular monitoring of how much you have in your bank and savings account. If you don't know precisely how much you have in your account, it is very hard to calculate an exact and reliable budget for the upcoming month. However, there's no need to worry; after reading this book and downloading the app, you will understand how to keep track of your finances.

Your balance

Check your balance and consider how much was deducted and for what. To give yourself a more accurate idea of how much you have in your account, you can often do several things to get a more accurate idea of your balance, such as:

- Asking for your balance over the phone.
- Checking your account online.
- Keeping track of your spending yourself.
- Going to your local branch or ATM.

Though you can always go to your bank and ask them how much is in your account, this isn't the most convenient way to find out your account balance since the bank may be closed when you need information. On the plus side, there are several ways to check your balance without going to the bank. A few of your options include:

- Accessing your bank account online.
- Getting a bank statement from an ATM (Automated Teller Machine).
- Checking your bank statements.
- Calling your bank to find out our balance.

Mindset on spending and saving

Everybody has their attitude to saving money. Many people save more than they spend, while others will spend their cash as soon as possible, without thinking about putting some aside for later. It's often easy to recognise these behavioural patterns in children.

Whether you consider yourself a spender or just someone who likes to use their hard-earned cash to treat themselves, it is crucial to know how to save money for when you'll really need it. Though your parents will make sure that you have all the essentials, there will be a day when you will have to look after yourself, so there's no better time to learn how to save than today!

Ways to spend money

After reading this topic, you'll have a better understanding of:

- Necessary spending
- Non-essential spending
- The different attitudes towards spending

Different expenses

First, we need to make a list of essential expenses, which usually range from bills to travel costs. Managing your finances to afford non-essentials can often be quite tricky. The challenging task can become even more complex if you have an irregular income stream or receive payments at different times. On top of all this, finding the best way to pay for something is another crucial factor to consider.

There are often several fees charged that you may not have even thought of, such as charges accrued when using a credit card. There are other fees, too, like the charge that comes with withdrawing cash from some ATM machines. While you won't have to pay an added fee on ATMs at a branch of your bank, the fixed-fee charge is likely to apply to any other ATMs, whether they're at another bank or in a store. Alongside these costs, there are many others, such as booking fees for holidays, hotels and theatres.

When trying to understand your finances and what you can and can't afford, it's vital to consider all these different factors and other potential costs before purchasing. This way, you can often find the best possible solution.

The difference between essentials and non-essentials

These terms are simple enough to understand. For example, essential expenses are things you need to pay and can encompass be a variety of things, but if you're living on your own, here are the most important ones that you'll need to consider:

- Electricity
- Cleaning products
- Food

- Gas

- Insurance

- Mobile phone

- TV license (applicable in many countries)

- Water

Your budget needs to adapt to changes

When it comes to managing your finances, while sticking to a budget can have a significant impact, changing your plans according to your circumstances is vital. For example, you may need to adjust your budget when your income changes one month, or one week, to another, to make sure that you set enough aside each week to put towards the overall monthly bill.

The additional importance of adjusting your budget is because a simple change in your income or essential expenses can impact your finances. So, to account for even the slightest of changes, it is well worth updating your budget to make sure that you have an accurate idea of what's going on with your money.

An example of this would be someone who doesn't earn a lot and might find a slight increase in their bills to be a significant difference. And if this is left unchanged in their budget, they could end up overspending without realising it.

Another instance that requires a budget change is when one of the income earners of the household loses their job since this can impact what you're able to afford (including the necessities). In these instances, it's essential to consider what luxuries you can miss out on, from eating out less to any other activities that cost money until your income picks back up again. Even then, there's a chance that your earnings will take a hit in the future, so you may have to reduce expenditure on non-essentials, at least for the time being.

There is a broad range of essential items and expenses that pretty much anyone will have to pay. If you're living with your parents, there's a chance they'll pay for these items on your behalf.

- Books
- Clothes
- Lunch
- Toiletries

- Transport

There are plenty of non-essential items that you don't need but might buy anyway, such as dining at restaurants, buying fashion accessories, or going to the cinema.

One thing that could help you is the budget rule. This simple plan divides spending into a ratio of 50/30/20. So, according to this plan, we spend 50% on necessities from our after-tax income. So, you'll need to pay a portion of your hard-earned cash to the government as tax payment (we'll get more into this later), 30% on the things we want and 20% for savings. For more information, download the mobile app or check our website.

Topic 5: Working

Nowadays, people want to be happy in the workplace and content with our jobs. Still, we can't always choose to work in a role that we enjoy. For example, if you were to ask a ploughman in Sherwood Forest if he liked his work, he probably wouldn't have said yes. Work is not always about doing something you enjoy, but more often about doing something necessary to earn money.

Around 120 years ago, people knew that you could choose your job. Kids would grow up and consider what they enjoyed doing and what they were good at, and pursue this dream instead. If your parents made horseshoes but your heart was destined to write poetry, you could aim to your make that goal a reality. Perhaps a young adult would have felt interested in joining the military while their parents pursued a more artistic occupation. Following your dream became a practical option as the world evolved.

In the modern world, we have a near-limitless range of opportunities in front of us. However, deciding on what career path to follow isn't always easy, especially for younger individuals who don't have a choice. In the past, children would follow in their parents' footsteps and continue within a family-run trade. For example, if they were sheep farmers, bakers or ferry owners at a lake crossing, their children would often follow suit, especially as they would pick up the skills needed for said trade from an early age. This can still be true in many countries worldwide, often where technology and the economy aren't as advanced. In more developed areas, continuing in the same line of work as your family can still happen. Still, it's often more of a choice than an expectation to do so.

Consider that you might go into another critical stage of life—starting an apprenticeship. As you change careers, you learn new skills and start to move forward, gradually improving upon the things you know along the way. In life, we can often feel insecure and forced to deal with various other emotional issues that will last a good while if we're don't confront them. While you still have time, it's essential to learn and gain information and experience from those wiser than you through an apprenticeship. In this process, you'll get new skills and become more independent and more equipped to deal with any challenges that come your way.

Most people today, especially the younger generation, are hopeful about their work and future. Even if you hear adults complaining about their job, it's good to know that most people try hard to enjoy their work or find a job that suits their passion. The idea of working for money alone sounds quite depressing, even if money is essential. You can certainly feel a sense of pride from earning money, but if you don't enjoy your work and it takes a toll on you and your happiness, it's not worth the cash. For most people, the ideal job is one that suits you and pays well.

The good news is that nowadays, this is achievable. Those who are good at their jobs and like what they do are far more likely to enjoy their day-to-day lives. You can't do a job well if you're not invested in the work that you do. If you're not enjoying it, it's often far harder to give it your all, which leads to less than perfect results.

Sure, jobs can be tedious, but they're a daily duty that we need to manage. Picking something that we like can help us be more productive and make a vast difference overall. but it will still eventually become repetitive and uninteresting. As an adult, your work shouldn't have to be boring, and working shouldn't have to be something that you dread doing, but many grown-ups usually end up doing a job that they don't like at some point in their working lives. You might find that you will have to as well, but there's still so many opportunities out there for you to move forward and find something you'll love further down the line.

Topic 5: Working

An excellent place to begin is to think of all the things that seem fun to you. This could be a variety of things, from playing games, sports, dressing up or spending time with your brother or sister—anything that you enjoy. Don't pay too much attention to how important it seems because as long as it's something you like, it's worth noting. Once you've got down the ideas, the next thing to do is consider what about the things that you like. You need to dig deeper into what brings you joy. What's the reason these things are so fun and engaging? People have different strengths; you may notice that other kids are better at certain subjects than you and maybe better at others. It's impossible to be the best at everything, so aiming to work with what you're already good at can be an excellent way to push you further in life.

It might help to do a brief thought experiment. Imagine being offered millions to work at a job that you hated, or instead earning the minimum wage (just enough to get by) for a job that you believe you would love doing. Which one seems better? For most, it's a simple choice. We can learn from this that earning a lot of cash and having a good job isn't the same. Many "good" jobs could be paid well but aren't enjoyable. Still, sometimes the jobs that pay less can be much more fulfilling for you to do, allowing you to enjoy yourself and help other people at the same time.

The downside to this is that the answer to this question isn't always straightforward. Though trying to find the right solution can often be frustrating and complicated, realising what to do with your working life is a huge decision that impacts two crucial factors in life—your happiness and the amount of money you earn.

For many people, it's simple to imagine a job that pays well in terms of money and dream of everything that can buy with the money earned, but it's easy to forget that you might spend most of your time doing something you don't enjoy. So, is the extra money worth it? Earning more cash is always good, but it's important to consider other aspects of your life, too. While searching for the right job for you, you'll need to make sure that you're making enough money and enjoying yourself at the same time.

Looking at how the world is today, we're fortunate to have the chance to earn money in a way that we like and can spend our lives doing something that we enjoy. But a more pressing issue has also arisen: what happens if you make the wrong choice? Going back to our earlier example, the ploughman in Sherwood Forest may not have been happy with his job. Still, he didn't have difficulty choosing which path was right for him, nor was there the trouble of picking the wrong job either.

Topic 5: Working

It's not uncommon for people to change jobs throughout their lives. Most people will have many varied jobs because job security isn't that great in today's economy. Of course, you may find the ideal industry work, but even then, there's no guarantee you'll keep that job. So, whether you leave because of necessity or your own choice, it's well worth keeping the following financial tricks in mind to help you with the transition:

- Be considerate of your spending.
- Try to maintain an emergency reserve fund.
- Think of the financial risks that can come with changing jobs.
- Before resigning, try to have a new job lined up.

Topic 6: Income

When you work for an employer, pay slips are issued weekly or monthly. Income is the money that you receive over a set period and can come from more than one source, such as:

- Employment

- Gift money

- Government benefits (while not given to everybody, this is money given to help certain people, like parents or disabled individuals).

- Pocket money

- Self-employed work

- Earning is the money you gain from doing a job. "To earn" is a verb that means getting something you have worked for, which is where the term earning comes from.

- Gross income, deductions, net income, and hours worked

- Net income and YTD (Year to date) income

- The hours worked to show the amount paid

Topic 6: Income

Earnings can often come in two forms: salary or wages.

- Wages — This term describes how much a person is paid per hour. Salaries are paid every week.

- Salary — This term describes a job's pay as a yearly figure (e.g. £15,000). This is written as per annum or pa, which is an easier way of writing it. A salary is often paid every month.

The payment for jobs is known as wages or salary, depending on what they are. Here are a few examples of jobs that offer income based on an hourly rate:

- Car park attendance
- Cleaning
- Farm work
- Gardening
- Temporary work
- Waiting tables

Examples of jobs that have a monthly payment that is referred to as a salary include:

- Call centre operative
- Cashier

- Government jobs
- Nurse or doctor
- Receptionist
- Secretary
- Teacher

In the modern world, we often perceive those with a lot of money as being good and those without it as being not as good. Without even realising it, we often use money to show how good a person is. It can be difficult for those in a tight position, but others will think the complete opposite—that the rich are bad and the poor are good—and this mindset isn't ideal either.

As we mentioned earlier, specialisation encouraged people to trade for goods and services, like a farmer trading food with a blacksmith for their metalworking skills.

What we can learn about the world of work is that not everyone is paid equally. For example, two people could work a similar amount of time and just as hard, yet one could make thousands upon thousands more—but why?

The good news is that the answer is simple. Just consider what a job is—you offer a service or product that you

Topic 6: Income

get rewarded in cash. Many people get paid more because not everyone does the same job, and not everyone is equally capable of the roles they undertake. Certain things can need more skill and ability, which not everyone can offer. Jobs can be much simpler and performed by a larger group of people, which has a significant influence on salary. The more in-demand a job is, the more it earns. A good sign of how good a job is to consider how much it's needed and how many other people can offer those services.

As mentioned earlier, a job that pays well can often bring to mind the different things you could buy. However, you could end up spending more time working than actually enjoying yourself. So, consider that wealth is not a reflection of how good or bad someone is; rather, it reflects how valuable and in-demand their work is.

Those who are self-employed work for themselves. A boss doesn't pay them a wage or salary but finds their work and earns money from their customers or clients. Painters, plumbers, and carpenters are just a few examples of self-employed workers. The money earned by self-employed individuals isn't referred to as either a salary or wages; in most cases, it is known as earnings or income.

Many people believe the world could be fairer, and by this they often mean that people should earn an equal amount of money; however, this isn't likely to change. Times change, and certain skills can increase in demand. For example, the 2000s was the era for mathematicians and computing engineers. But unlike the world that Robin Hood lived in, we depend so much on technology that it's unlikely to change. Technology will continue to evolve, but it is not the only example we can use. For example, the essential skills in Sherwood Forest involved architecture and stone masonry. Although those skills are crucial today, they are not as sought after as computer technology and artificial intelligence.

Key Terms

- *Employee*: Most adults have a job and earn money from their work. An employer is someone who provides the job, and likewise, employees are individuals who work for someone else. This can apply to various jobs, from a company to the government. Employees will often receive a salary payment for the work they do.

- *Self-employed*: an individual who owns a business is likely to earn their money by working for themselves as opposed to under someone else. Most people call them self-employed individuals or business owners because they have to make money from

Topic 6: Income

their ventures rather than pay an employer. To earn a profit from their work, they need to calculate their income and outgoings. Their income is the revenue that comes from selling their services/goods, and outgoings are expenses that cover the costs of providing said services and interests (such as materials, the wages of their employees and much more).

If you want to test your knowledge on the matter, be sure to head over to *www.sherwoodfinance.com* or download the Sherwood Finance app and follow us on YouTube.

Topic 7: Savings

The tale of Robin Hood is still around today, but the world was much different back then. He and his merry men didn't need a good job or financial security. Still, most of us will need good savings plans and considerations to live. One example of this is how the pandemic has affected so many individuals, and how, even if we're prepared for the unknown, we can't predict what will happen. However, we can still put in a little effort now to protect ourselves in an unsavoury event—and the sooner we save, the better. Sure, everyone likes a treat, but waiting so you can save up for something more significant, or for unforeseen circumstances, can often be a far better idea.

You'll find that there are multiple kinds of saving accounts, as well as different companies that offer them. So, when you save, you need to know that there are plenty of options and consider what each one could do for you.

Suppose you store your earnings in a savings account. In that case, you'll earn interest on it, meaning that the bank or organisation you're putting your money into will pay you a small percentage. When saving your money at a bank, you're lending them that cash. The bank or building society will use your money (entrusted by other savers) to offer loans to people who will pay the money back and the extra interest cost. After researching and getting advice from experienced people, you earn money from the stock market.

When you consider spending your savings or income, remember these two words and what they mean.

Assets or Liabilities

As a company that focuses on improving financial literacy, we do not define assets or liabilities in the traditional way. If you want to be confused, look up the words in a dictionary as the definitions make little sense on their own.

These terms are not words that characterise assets and liabilities but numbers, so you need to understand them. Whether you work, property is an asset if it can generate income or appreciation. Liabilities are things that drain your pockets, either by depreciating or by taking money from your income like a car loan.

What often happens is many young adults tend to take on liabilities before buying assets, so it is important not to make the mistake of believing that making more money will solve the problem, since it can worsen the situation.

Money often exposes our human flaws by shedding light on what we do not know. If anyone has heard of those tales in which somebody receives money because of inheritance or lottery, in no time at all, their financial situation could be worse than before they received the money. The simplest explanation is that their spending pattern stays the same, only they are spending more money. A fool and his or her money are easily parted, as the old saying goes.

It is not uncommon for doctors or lawyers to experience financial difficulties, and people from other walks of life can also experience spending problems. Awareness is the first step to overcome these difficulties. Many young people who leave school without financial acumen pursue successful careers, only to struggle financially; they work harder, but still cannot get ahead with their finances. Often, it's not financial acumen, work ethic, or even a good grasp of maths that is missing from their education, but a lack of information on how to manage earnings and debts.

What you do once you have earned the money, how you keep people from being able to take it, how you keep it longer and how you turn it into an asset are skills that aren't taught enough in schools. Cash flow is a concept that most people do not understand, which leads to their financial struggles. There are many people that have developed skills in a certain field yet still experience financial struggles. Since they have learned how to behave in a work environment to earn, but not how to make their money work for them, these people often work harder than they need too.

To learn more, download the Sherwood finance app at the Google Play store.

What is a cash flow forecast?

In simple terms, a cash flow forecast calculation that helps you understand future events and their effect on your finances. It's a plan to help you figure out how much money will go in and come out of your account. A cash flow forecast can help you better understand how much you can afford to spend on non-essential items, which is why it can be such a great tool.

Deficit and Surplus

Two words associated with budgeting are surplus and deficit. Here's what they mean:

- Surplus is excess money. When you create and follow a budget, you will often have a surplus at the end of the week/month.

- The deficit is the amount overspent. A typical example of this is when you spend all the cash in your current account and open an overdraft.

Is your money safe?

One of the main reasons so many people leave their money in a savings account is that it is far safer and more secure than being left sitting around at home.

Banks will only keep a set amount of money, but they will always return your money. So, if there were a "run on the bank," as it's called, where many people all withdraw money at once, the government would make sure that everyone gets the right amount of cash.

This sounds good, but what happens if a bank goes bust?

The UK government guarantees up to £85,000 of savings per person. Not only is it unlikely for banks to go bust, but the government has a plan in place to compensate for the lost money (or at least a large portion of it). You could save money in different accounts since each person will be covered by £85,000 from each provider. It's unlikely that multiple banks and building societies will all go bust at once.

What would happen if a bank was robbed?

Well, if someone robs a bank, can the bank still pay you back without issue? Today, the majority of our money is electronic and moved around via digital transfers.

Since a wage or salary is paid to your account, we often use direct debit to pay the bills, and since many of us make purchases via debit card anyway, physical cash has become far less prominent. So, if money is stolen, it's likely to only be an insignificant amount in the grand scheme of things.

Good or bad, most individuals learn their financial habits from a young age and from the surrounding people during childhood. For those who know little about sound financial practices, here are a couple of helpful tips:

▶ Every month, never spend more than the amount of money you earn.

▶ Instead of searching for the best price, look for the best value.

▶ Buying from a brand doesn't always guarantee high-quality goods.

▶ Keep track of and collect your refunds.

- Try to limit any needless spending habits or cut back on pricier things.

- Avoid personal loans and credit cards.

Remember that your money can grow over time because of the interest earned when deposited in a bank. In these cases, interest is the money that the bank pays you so that they can use your money for their investments. So, when you deposit your money, you're allowing them to use it for their business while still having access to it and the additional amount given to you in interest.

How do lenders calculate interest?

This is just a brief look at how banks can make money from depositors and borrowers. First, it might be worth noting that rates are not fixed for the entire loan length. Rates often change over time because of different factors. In the year 2000, for example, certain banks were paying interest rates of up to five per cent to depositors, while borrowers had to deal with higher interest rates on their loans. While this wasn't ideal, the banks needed to profit. Nowadays, banks pay little interest in savings. But here is how it works. The claim that you can earn from the money in your savings account is a percentage of how much is in there each year, added to your savings balance. If it's left there, you'll receive more interest with

Topic 7: Savings

each year that passes, and your savings will continue to grow.

As a young adult, it may seem that you need to make as much money as possible. However, as we discussed in the earlier chapter, you can see that it can be better to earn less money for something more fulfilling. So, while we need money to pay for essential items to live, money itself isn't the most crucial thing in the world.

So, you might wonder how much money is enough. We assume that having more money than we need is a good thing, and while this can seem obvious, it's not always the case. What you need to consider is *why* this is an accepted concept. Many believe that the more money you have, the more remarkable your life will be, but this is far from the truth. In fact, the amount of money you have isn't as connected to happiness as you may think. It may be necessary, but how much can having extra money improve your life? Take into consideration that a higher-paying job could be far less enjoyable. Then, the answer may become a little clearer.

Going out to dinner is a good example of this. While not so important to kids, how much to spend on eating out is something that an adult will consider. On the one hand, you could opt for a cheaper restaurant, where the food may not be as exciting and the area itself may not be as luxurious. On the other hand, you could spend more money enjoying a meal somewhere with more elaborate dishes and a better atmosphere. It's easy to see which one is the preferred experience.

Of course, as mentioned above, most people think that it's better to go to the more expensive restaurant, and in that case, it's better to have more money; however, this won't be true for everybody when going to a cheaper restaurant. Let's imagine you went with a few friends and had a great time together, chatting and feeling good about the time you've spent together. Overall, a night with the good friends can be more worthwhile than eating tasty food. In contrast, if you go to a fancy establishment with someone you don't know too well or even on your own, the experience would be less memorable.

When we receive or have money, we can spend it or save it as we see fit. And, while we need to spend money on things that we need, it is essential to make sure that we save up for more considerable expenses in the future, such as a car, house, or higher education. Besides this, saving money can help you prepare for emergencies or unexpected expenses that could occur down the line.

What is exciting about money is that it can grow when put in the right place. This is called investing. No matter how old you are, you can support your savings and earn even more money—and the sooner you start, the larger it can grow.

Better yet, even outside of spending, saving, and investing money, there's also the financial power to help the community. Having money allows you to support charities or make a difference in the lives of others. There's no better feeling than contributing to a worthy cause and helping someone, and you'll learn more about this later.

Because of the opportunities that money can open for us, we often dream of having a lot. But the main issue is that getting money isn't always the easiest of tasks. Perhaps you've heard the expression "money doesn't grow on trees"—a statement that illustrates that earning money isn't as simple as just picking it up off the ground.

The less than ideal realities deal with money. For example, if someone buys more than they can afford, they'll end up in negative numbers and must deal with debt. Not just that, but people can lose money if they put their hard-earned savings into the wrong investments. If you don't learn to manage or protect your money correctly, there's a chance that you'll lose it. In addition, if you don't have money available, you can get stressed about getting into debt and about not having enough to buy what you need. As you can see, with so many difficulties, it's easy for people to worry about their finances.

Because of this, taking care of your income is a responsibility you can't take for granted. This is where having financial knowledge is vital. Finance is managing money, and learning such skills are crucial for earning and saving later. It'll give you a better understanding of how money works and help you make better financial decisions as you spend, save, and invest. There's no better time to learn about finance than the present, but we'll get more into that in the following chapters.

When considering your financial position, it's essential to consider how we manage the money that we need to spend—and this is a necessary part of budgeting. Everybody needs to figure out how to pay the sum they have at their disposal. For example, it's not such a good idea to spend all the cash you've earned in a week on entertainment when the money is needed for essentials.

The necessities can include a wide variety of things, from buying food to paying back the money you owe. Anything that you need to do comes under essentials—these are the things that are a must. Next up, you need to consider the money you set aside for your wants.

Though not essential to your survival, all these things

Topic 7: Savings

can improve your quality of life, such as going out to dinner, electronic gadgetry and anything else that may not be essential but still nice to have. So, for example, you don't need the latest iPhone, and you could cook something at home instead of eating out, but if you put money aside, then you'll feel much better about treating yourself from time to time.

When it comes to saving up for a house or even an investment property, it would be best to aim to have at least 10% left over to save or invest. All these saving tips are excellent way to help you build up a nice sum of money for later in life.

Many young adults are better at saving than others. Those who put money aside will often have developed good financial habits from their parents. Many good savers are motivated towards achieving financial goals like buying a property, retiring young, starting their own company and much more. However, reaching these benchmarks is often far more difficult for those who spend more money than necessary.

For more information about saving your money, head over to www.sherwoodfinance.com or download the app at the Google Play store.

Topic 8: Taxes

Taxes have been around for centuries, dating back to the earliest human civilisations. it is worth looking closer into taxes because of their importance today and throughout history. We can see the first income tax records in the Egyptian Era and in Roman times. The Romans introduced public taxes, where the more someone owned, the more they pay. In 10 AD in China, Emperor Wang Mang introduced a different tax with a charge of 10 per cent on profits for professionals and workers.

In Sherwood Forest, the story goes that Richard the Lionheart was using taxes from Britons to finance the battle of the crusades. Since the taxes were not going back to the people of Britain, the citizens suffered. It is said that the sheriff of Sherwood Forest was more of a tyrant than the king by enforcing unaffordable taxes, and so started the story of Robin Hood. When citizens pay taxes, the world is a much safer place, so everyone must pay taxes based on their earnings. In short, we give a percentage of our money to the government to improve our quality of life.

Governments use income tax for various things, such as providing education and healthcare. There are so many

Topic 8: Taxes

services that our tax money goes into funding. What else can you think of that those taxes pay for?

We don't have to pay taxes on everything we earn. Everybody can earn up to a set amount without being charged tax. This is called a personal allowance. When you earn more than this, you will be taxed on a percentage of the amount that exceeds the personal budget. This is called income tax.

If you look a little into taxes, you'll find that they're likely to be one of your most significant expenses in life, alongside payments like housing costs. Because of this, consider how you can reduce your taxes (within the boundaries of the law, of course). In addition, understanding the laws and regulations can help you make sure that you don't get charged with unwanted penalties.

Everybody must pay taxes. The money collected from the tax goes toward paying for various things, from roads to schools. In addition, the tax system allows the government to collect funds from citizens to make the community better.

The tax office assesses your taxable income annually. In the UK, employees will pay taxes through the PAYE (Pay-As-You-Earn) system when paying taxes. The tax office gives employers tables to calculate how much tax is due from each employee, which they will then deduct from their wages to pay it down. In addition, each employee has a tax code, which employers can use to make sure that the right amount of tax is deducted from their workers. This code shows how much the employee can earn without paying tax and considers different adjustments, exemptions and allowances.

The terms and other factors can often change depending on where you live, but the overall system is similar in most parts of the world. Self-employed people pay their taxes to the tax office at a rate based on their net profits from their accounts (including those in a business partnership). Since they are both used to decide the amount of income tax a person owes, net profits are the equivalent of an employee's gross income. Net profits are calculated both with capital allowances and allowable business expenses against the business's total income. Taxpayers need to find out their liability and send these figures for approval. While there are differences between the UK, the US and Australia, the system is similar. Knowing your taxable income is essential because it can help you understand how to reduce it (within legal bounds) when working out your income tax return for each financial year.

To test your knowledge on taxes, head over to www.sherwoodfinance.com or download the app at the Google Play store.

Topic 8: Insurance

Back in Sherwood Forest, no system could help protect your finances. If the tyrannical king and his soldiers burned down your home, your only means of transport, or if your horse's leg broke, there was no means of insurance to help you cover it; however, the good news is that today, we can pay for insurance to help cover the costs if we need them. Thanks to the fact that you've been paying a small monthly fee to them, you'll be able to call your insurance provider and deal with the high prices with ease.

The earliest insurance was a more primitive version of commercial insurance and was originally intended for transporting goods (since cargo can be lost, damaged or stolen by thieves). However, overall, the original form of insurance helped reduce the risks involved with transferring items, allowing businesses to run more smoothly.

Nowadays, there's insurance for just about everything. Undoubtedly, the most important form of insurance is health insurance. If you are still young and living with family, you're unlikely to be concerned with health insurance. No matter your age. Many people get their health insurance through their employer, but they don't have the coverage. Studies prove that one in five people in their 20s lacks health insurance.

When a homeowner's house burns down and they don't have house insurance, most people cannot afford to rebuild the property and replace the furniture and items lost in the destruction.

While a rare occurrence, a house fire is always a possibility, so it's a risk you shouldn't be willing to take. Most homebuyers choose to take out an insurance policy, which protects them from the likelihood of such dangers. The insurance policy is an agreement where the property owner will pay the insurance company a set amount each year. In addition, they will pay for the rebuilding of the house should you need it. Of course, this can't prevent a home from burning to ashes, but it provides financial protection at the very least.

If you buy a home through a mortgage loan, the lender will encourage you to get homeowner's insurance. This is a reasonable decision as a lender will want to make sure that their investment in the property is protected (and you should want to protect your stake, too). It would be best to take out homeowner's insurance because it protects your property and offers liability insurance should anything happen or if legal issues arise.

Topic 8: Insurance

There are many unforeseen ways you or anybody else could lose money; for example, through natural disasters, hurricanes or earthquakes, or through medical problems or car accidents—these issues can come with a hefty cost to mend.

One example of coverage you may need in the future is family life insurance. With this policy, you'll need to make payments monthly to an insurer to protect your family if anything happens to you.

You may wonder what happens if you pass away while still paying for this insurance. In these instances, your insurer intends to pay a sum of money you agreed upon when you took the policy out, known as the sum insured, to your beneficiary. This can either be in monthly instalments or one lump sum.

If you investigate, you'll see that there's insurance for everything. Depending on your current circumstances, specific packages could be better than others. Those living in Sherwood Forest never protected themselves against issues like natural disasters. It's just one of many luxuries in the modern world. Here are a few examples of the different types of coverage available:

- Motor vehicle insurance
- Building insurance

- Health insurance
- Home insurance
- Pet insurance
- Travel insurance

For more facts and tips on insurance, check out our website at www.sherwoodfinance.com

Topic 9: Borrowing

Credit

There are quite a few ways a lender can offer credit services to their clients, such as student loans, auto loans, mortgages or credit cards. Even utility companies offer credit services, too. For example, in your own home, you likely use credit when you turn on the light, surf the internet, or use your phone (as a few examples). A utility company gives credit to your parents for the services that you use daily, and your parents pay for how much they use later. Aside from what you may think credit means, it can mean something else. In financial terms, to give someone credit is to lend them money.

There are many advantages to credit. For example, when someone doesn't have enough money, they can use credit to help them get the cash they need and pay off their debts when they're in a better position later. Credit can also allow individuals to borrow money against their expected future income. This can be great for more expensive purchases, such as education, homes, or cars. We can use credit for many things and give fresh opportunities to those who would otherwise go without.

When borrowing money, an individual will later need to pay for the following:

- The amount they borrowed.

- The interest, which is determined by a percentage of the amount borrowed.

- Any additional fees that the lender charges.

Retail and wholesale banking

Size is the key difference between retail and wholesale transactions, with the former being much smaller than the latter. Most end-users of our retail services are small businesses and individuals, where wholesale banking is often far more common among larger companies, as well as other big organisations and financial institutions.

Retail transactions are targeted toward personal and small corporate clients, often comprising services such as loans and deposits. These types of banking needs are often taken out by building societies and high-street banks, delivering their products through the internet, call centres or branch networks. In most cases, these financial institutions act as the bridge between people who want a loan and those who have funds they're willing to deposit. As you're likely to already know,

Topic 9: Borrowing

borrowing often comes with a price tag, which we all know as *interest*.

Wholesale banking is raising money via wholesale money markets where financial institutions (as well as large companies) can buy and sell assets. When financing houses, for example, this is the best method to go with—and many retail banks are involved with wholesale banking to top up deposits from branch networks when necessary.

A good example of this is when a bank makes a profitable loan but doesn't quite have the right deposits to take it on board. In these cases, they can raise the money they need via wholesale transactions.

It's important to note that wholesale banking operations are riskier than retail ones. After the crisis between 2007 and 2009, regulators ensured banks involved with retail and wholesale transactions didn't expose a retail client's deposits to any potential risks during their wholesale operations.

Subprime lenders

There are many individuals out there who struggle to meet the criteria of most mainstream lending institutes. These borrowers:

- Are outside of the typical borrower profile because of their form of income, residency, occupation, age, etc.

- Are self-employed and don't have the required accounts from earlier years or a short track record in the industry.

- Don't have proof of a different income.

- Have a bad credit history, caused by either payment defaults or court judgements.

While borrowers who don't meet the standard criteria imposed by lending institutions don't have to mean a bad business proposition, it can require taking a different route and considering specialised solutions. While lenders will often charge higher interest on loans that come with higher risk (or the 'rate for risk,' as it's often called), they may find it worthwhile.

What is a mortgage?

The bank has been lending people money to buy properties for hundreds of years. To make their money back, they charge an additional amount on top of the mortgage from the day of settlement. This extra money is known as interest and added to the loan you take out, but it is not hidden or added without warning. You'll get a statement notifying you of the amount you owe and how much paid so far. If you don't keep up with your payments, your lender will call you and chase you up, and perhaps even charge a fee if this is the case. This will happen between 15 to 30 days after receiving a statement. The lender may increase interest to the default charges listed in the loan agreement.

In simple terms, mortgages are loans that use an asset as collateral. When purchasing a house, they use the property as security. A mortgage can be, for example, taken out on share portfolios. When a loan is secured, it gives the lender the right over the asset until the loan is repaid. This way, lenders can relax in the knowledge that even if their borrower defaults on their payments, they can still get their money back by selling the asset.

Remember that not everyone who tries to get a mortgage will succeed. Banks will work with people they believe are most reliable and likely to pay the money back.

But how do they decide who qualifies? Several factors often come into play when deciding the reliability of an applicant, from their income to family size. Here's an in-depth look into the critical factors banks pay close attention to:

How lenders assess the loan application

Character — This refers to the borrower's reputation and willingness to repay the owed money. A person's character encompasses various things, like work experience and credit score.

The lender or bank will review the applicant's credit report when someone applies for credit. This report can show the lender the potential borrower's credit history, including their track record of paying back debts and the debt they still owe.

Capacity — A term for the borrower's ability to repay the loan. When individuals apply for a loan, the bank will investigate their income and how stable their job is if they owe money on any other loans, as well as how much they have been paid back if there are other debts. Having a decent-sized income and a stable job is a good sign that the borrower will make regular payments on time.

Topic 9: Borrowing

The lender will assess a potential borrower's employment conditions (e.g. the length of their current employment, prior experience and whether they are employed on a full-time, part-time or casual basis). Self-employed individuals are assessed differently. To decide the amount you can borrow, lenders will consider your income, assets and liabilities, as well as how many credit cards are in use, how much cash is stored in savings, and if these things are suitable/typical for the applicant's age.

Before buying, you might need to take out a property inspection, and while sellers will allow extensions, it is not a guarantee. Getting a pre-approval could be a great way to avoid this hassle.

The term credit is an agreement whereby a borrower can get something valuable for paying it back in small payments (with interest) until the total price is paid. Credit allows a borrower to get services or products they need and have the chance to enjoy its benefits immediately, while slowing down payment to make it more manageable. Anything that a borrower receives through credit must be repaid. The total amount delivered through credit will often be higher than the original price because of the additional interest expense.

Businesses can use credit for growth and expansion. For example, by using credit, a company can buy the supplies and materials they need, even if they only have petty cash to spare. They could even use credit for much larger purchases to buy equipment, vehicles and even new property. This can lead to more profit to sweeten the deal, allowing them to pay off their loans more quickly. Then, there is much more to go through when the time is right, such as which type of interest we should apply for.

The government can use credit for large projects to improve roads, bridges and buildings. They are taken care of with credit and thanks to tax. The government can often collect the cash they need to pay off the loan while improving the community for taxpayers. As mentioned earlier, tax is necessary to pay for various government projects, from the police and armed forces to schools and hospitals.

Secured lending

With any form of secured loan, a borrower offers something of value (e.g. a business asset) as security for the lender. This way, if the individual defaults on their payments, the lender takes and sells the asset and is repaid from the proceeds.

As you may guess, the most common form of secured personal lending is the mortgage loan for a house—with the item at stake being the borrower's home. When the property value increases, it is not uncommon for people to borrow against the increased equity. They may, for example, take out a further loan from their mortgage lender (a further advance), arrange a second mortgage from a different lender or re mortgage a larger amount. Then, they can use the loan to fund purchases that aren't related to their mortgage but still improve their way of living.

Bridging finance is sometimes required to help fill a funding gap that arises when the borrower relies on the sale of a property that hasn't gone through yet. In a secured loan, the house is the security, even where the loan itself isn't connected to the house purchase.

Second mortgages

If a borrower offers the property for a second time as security while the original lender still has a mortgage secured on it, it is classed as a second mortgage. In these instances, a lender will take a second charge on the property and the first one will keep the deeds (this charge takes precedence over the following charges).

If the borrower defaults on their payments, the original lender's claim will first be met in full, and if enough money remains, the second mortgage's charge will be met later. A lender is only likely to offer a second mortgage if there is enough equity and if the individual accepts a higher interest rate than that of their first loan, since second mortgages come with a higher risk.

Unsecured lending

In contrast to secured loans, an unsecured loan relies on the borrower's personal promise, or covenant, to repay. Unsecured loans imply a higher risk than secured lending. They have higher interest rates and are only available for shorter terms. For example, while a mortgage secured on a property will be available for 25 years or even longer, we offer an unsecured loan over much over six or seven years. A few examples of such loans are described below.

Car Loans

Buying a car with credit for the future isn't a good idea, because it isn't a necessary expense at your age and your income is not likely to be sufficient. In addition, there are essential factors to consider; for example, that you shouldn't be expected to have one right now or that they can be costly to keep.

Even if you don't use credit to buy one, there will still be a variety of other expenses to keep in mind. For example, in some parts of the world, you can get around just fine without a car, and you could save a decent amount of cash by taking the bus or train. However, if you need a car, our best advice would be to save your money and not take out a loan. And you should also consider the ongoing costs that will come with it, such as:

- Auto insurance
- Fuel
- General maintenance
- Government registration

Personal loans

You can get money by taking out a loan from a financial institution. All loans should be used for a specific purpose, such as buying a house or car.

Personal loans are one of many ways you can borrow cash, with varying loan periods set in the agreement. You could, for example, ask for £1,000 and pay it off over a year, or as high as £10,000 with a duration that gives you several years to pay it back. Borrowers will have to put in a little time to find a payment period that best suits their needs. In most cases, monthly repayments on these loans are fixed and will have the same interest rate throughout.

Loans offer much more significant amounts of money than overdrafts do. This is because overdrafts are made to be small, often for a few hundred pounds over a month. A loan will be for thousands and have much longer loan terms, sometimes lasting a year (or as long as 10).

When considering the costs of personal loans, lenders should tell you how many monthly repayments will costand this, as well as the total loan amount, won't change.

Credit cards

A credit card can allow you to buy something and pay for it later. They can be used for most services and goods in stores, paying for food at restaurants and a variety of other in-person payments and withdrawing money (although this comes with a fee). You can use credit cards to buy services and goods online, by mail or over the phone.

At the end of each month, cardholders receive a statement listing all the transactions they've made and how much they come to. They can then choose to pay this amount off in its entirety, or a part of it first and the rest later. Those who pay it all off don't have to pay

Topic 9: Borrowing

interest; however, those who only pay part of the amount they owe will be charged interest on the remaining cash.

When taking out a loan or using a credit card, you must always consider the amount you'll have to pay as interest. However, if you use a credit card to pay off the balance as soon as you receive the statement, there won't be any interest. It only becomes an issue when you leave the debt, even if you pay it off, as the provider will charge you extra based on a percentage of what you owe. You're charged more interest for the longer your debt is left unpaid when using an overdraft.

Something you might not know is that some retailers and stores will have a transaction charge when paying by credit card. This is often the same case when buying stuff online. While this fee will only be a small percentage of the overall purchase, it still adds up and can end up being more money spent.

In these situations, individuals need to make a minimum repayment that's at least equal to a single month's interest. This means that cardholders need to first pay off the interest, followed by the outstanding amount. Those who only make the minimum repayments will find it much more challenging to pay off their debt in the future.

When you use a credit card, you're borrowing money

from the card company. Cardholders have a 'credit limit', which is the highest amount they can withdraw.

Business borrowers

When a mortgage is taken for business and secured on a business premises, the loan isn't considered a regulated mortgage.

In a standard, regulated mortgage, lenders need to see the business plan, or at least evidence that the loan is intended for business and the decision is often based on the income and outgoings of the applicant, much like with regular loans. When a loan is repaid by business resources, it's necessary for a lender to know how strong these resources are.

In these instances, the borrower is reliant on their business for personal income and covering any mortgage payments, even if they increase in the future. Because of this, lenders will want to make sure that the business can support the costs of the loan, as well as other expenditures (such as the necessities).

Interest rates on loans

Interest rates vary on different loans, the main difference being secured or unsecure, or in other words, whether the lender has any tangible assets to recover if the loan is not repaid. Remember that unsecured loans are riskier and come with higher charges with lending. It is a common misconception that banks earn a lot of cash; they can only make so much because of the interest they charge on their loans. The interest rate is a charge for borrowing money so that the lender can make a profit, worked out by how much you take out and other factors. As a result, they state interest as a cost over each year. The term used is per annum.

To calculate the amount charged, you need the overall amount of money, including the principal or capital, the annual interest rate and the term of the loan. Without a mathematical calculator, you won't get the capital amount, so if you wish to make a simulation, head over to our website at www.sherwoodfinance.com

Fixed or Variable

Choosing between variable and fixed-rate loans is critical. Before buying a home, be sure to weigh up each mortgage's advantages and disadvantages. Each has its pros and cons; the important considerations are whether a fixed or variable rate will be ideal for your needs.

If you want more certainty, apply for a fixed rate. A fixed rate will allow you to fit your repayments into your budget without having to worry about any interest fluctuations.

While most lenders have a buffer and review your living expenses before offering finance, when the interest rate increases, property owners may struggle to meet the requirements of their higher monthly repayments.

When considering variable rate loans, you may make unlimited contributions to your mortgage. In contrast, fixed-rate repayments are capped per annum, and how much varies with the lender.

For a quiz about purchasing real estate, head over to www.sherwoodfinance.com

Overdraft

An overdraft is a unique way of borrowing money from your current account. You can get an overdraft from local financial institutes, who will decide your overdraft limit (the amount you can borrow). When you spend over these limits, the bank will open an allowed or arranged

Topic 9: Borrowing

overdraft. Keep in mind that extra charges come with setting up an overdraft.

Issuing a cheque without having enough money to cover it (or other ways of borrowing without permission from the bank) is known as an unauthorised overdraft. The bank will pay the cheque, but they'll charge you for it as a reprimand for not checking if you can borrow before taking out more than you own. An overdraft can let you withdraw more money from your bank account than what is there. So, even if you only have £50, you can still withdraw £60. By doing so, you're taking out an overdraft.

Topic 10: Credit reporting

Credit files didn't exist back in the time of Sherwood Forest, and it is only in recent years that they've become so advanced. Credit can be helpful to many people, but it comes with risks. Whatever you borrow you must pay back in the future, with regular payment schedules and deadlines, which must be adhered to. The difficulty lies in those who don't use credit correctly and allow their debt to spiral out of control. Plus, since you will be charged interest, the amount you owe could add up to more than you can handle. Overspending can put borrowers in a challenging situation when they can't keep up with their repayments, which, if not paid, could lead to the loss of valuable items, such as a car, or even a house. If you fall back on your payments, it's going to cost you big time. And it gets worse, too—if you cannot pay back loans, it can have a massive impact on your reputation as a borrower. In many cases, too much credit can often lead to family problems and other relationship-related issues, and in some parts of the world, it can also lead to jail time or bankruptcy.

Be aware that comprehensive credit reporting can change the outcome when making lending decisions. This means that if you're a good borrower, it's recorded

Topic 10: Credit reporting

on your credit report, which will show your credit score. This rates how borrowers have managed their past loans and the number of loans they still need to pay off. Borrowers with over one or two late repayments will have a lower score. Having too many loans can reduce it further. When lenders decide to offer money, your credit score will often be a significant deciding factor for a bank. The higher the credit score, the better chances of getting approval. And in most cases, better scores earn lower interest rates. In contrast, lower scores can either have higher interest rates or be rejected.

Because of this, taking care of your credit reputation and keeping a high score is vital. If you end up struggling with debt now, it could cause you issues far into the future, if you ever need to apply for loans.

How can you improve your credit score?

- Try not to avoid unnecessary use of credit
- Pay off your debts as you go
- Aim to make your payments on time

We can't stress how important your financial affairs are, and if you're not careful, the impact of mismanaged finances will last for years, preventing you from getting credit, costing you extra and making it harder for you to advance. Consider the following scenario: Suppose you cannot settle the outstanding debt and a creditor files a bill on your credit report. In that case, they're likely to contact the people they need to list the debt, which will remain visible for five years. So, what's the good news in all this? The bank may make exceptions in certain instances, especially if it's a small amount of debt—although this will need to be paid before you can get approval.

To test your knowledge on your credit file, check out our website at: www.sherwoodfinance.com

Bankruptcy?

Bankruptcy is a legal concept that must be avoided at all costs. Known as Insolvency, bankruptcy arises when a person's liabilities exceed their assets or if a person cannot meet their financial obligations within a reasonable time. Bankruptcy goes one step further when someone's insolvent financial position is formalised under a bankruptcy order. Changes have been made over the years, though the principle is essentially the same. In 2002, an EU regulation was introduced on Insolvency Proceedings and statutory instruments, and

Topic 10: Credit reporting

the Insolvency (Amendment) Rules 2002 were issued to solidify its position in the United Kingdom.

If an individual or business cannot repay the money they owe, the individual or company still has a chance to start again by forgiving their debts but declaring bankruptcy, which has long-lasting effects. A declaration of bankruptcy will be recorded on your credit file, which could prevent you from taking out new loans or, at the least, increase the interest rates you get on them. Filing for bankruptcy can be a complex and expensive process and can have an additional impact on gaining employment, since it could encourage an employer to hire a candidate with a better track record and handling of their finances.

An individual or business can petition for bankruptcy or be demanded by a creditor to declare the person bankrupt if they owe more than £5,000 (even if the amount is owed between multiple debtors). These orders will remain in force for a year. After that, the individual is undischarged bankrupt, where they will have to follow the terms. During this period, the person's possessions can be surrendered to the official receiver, who can take the items and sell them to pay back creditors.

The only exceptions are clothing, household items and work-related items. However, bankruptcy cancels most debts and allows people to make a fresh financial start. It comes at a price: bankruptcy makes it more difficult to get credit in the future, which, in turn, affecting employment prospects. Bankrupts cannot borrow, other than nominal amounts, during the period order is in force. An undischarged bankrupt cannot open a current account. Still, it may open a basic bank account. Even after the period, the person must, by law, disclose the existence of bankruptcy when applying for a mortgage. This may mean that it will be more difficult for them to get a loan or be charged a higher interest rate to cover the greater perceived risk.

For more tips on avoiding bankruptcy, head to www.sherwoodfinance.com or download the app from the Google Play store and follow us on YouTube.

Conclusion

Many people before us have said that the mind is where our plans are made. A mix of action and desire forms in our imagination, and after deciding what to pursue in life, you must maintain an everlasting persistence until every resource has been tested. so, it is essential to develop your curiosity and willingness to learn. Without it, you may not gain much information or skill, and it can often be a challenge to go far without knowledge, skill or experience.

Remember that an excellent education is far more than going to college, and that learning should be a regular part of your life. We can always learn from our environment, and the more you know, the more options you have. You might even find purpose to your life! Regardless, more than ever, today's world requires us to be capable of communication. Of course, reading and writing are essential skills that can create a variety of opportunities. Still, the constant changing world presents challenges, and the next generation will create a new vision. One of the world's most famous and enduring stories, the story of Robin Hood has been illustrated to show how the world has changed, but it is also a story that represents resistance, and I'm afraid these stories of resistance will continue because what defines wrongful authority and what rules supports rebellion behaviour. The answer is a mystery. Whether or not you believe in Nelson Mandela or Greta Thunberg, they created a following by speaking out, and it took strength and conviction to carry on, but then they changed the world through learning how to communicate and by sharing their vision.

Regardless of what you want from life, the time we have is limited, and you may not have unlimited resources to get what you want—but the learning opportunities are endless. Though there's never been a better time in our existence for seeking knowledge, so much time can be wasted trying to do it alone. Instead, it's far better to save yourself time by looking for a mentor where you can hone your skills and be guided in the right direction. As a result, you will learn much faster from their feedback.

We wish you luck in the future, and as you find your way through life, don't forget to plan your goals, reflect on them and measure your successes and pitfalls. Given the wealth of online options available, albeit only from credible sources, it is well worth looking into current financial advice and information. We hope you enjoyed looking into the beginner's world of finances, and if you want to test your understanding of anything we've gone through or get advice on financial matters, be sure to download our app from the Google Play store.

Conclusion

Here are a few other things that you should put into practice in your daily life:

- Healthy habits
- Maintaining good relationships
- Being thankful for everything you have
- Be mindful of your reputation
- Look out for learning opportunities
- Enjoying yourself and having fun
- Taking care of your family
- Stating your goals in writing

Head over to our website at www.sherwoodfinance.com or download the Sherwood Finance app.

Glossary

Apprenticeship.

Training involves learning from someone experienced in a trade. Apprenticeships are essential learning platforms for carpenters, doctors and many other professionals as one of the best ways to learn trade skills is with an expert.

Arrangement fees.

When lenders charge for the effort of providing financing to a borrower. Fees can vary from one lender to another.

ATM/Cash machine.

Money that is withdrawn from a bank account via machine.

Auction.

Overseen by an auctioneer, an auction is a public sale of goods or property to the highest bidder.

Auctioneer.

A professional who oversees the sale of real estate or other items whereby persons become purchasers by competition in public view.

Glossary

Balance.

A statement begins with your last statement's balance, which is the amount you had in your account at the end of the most recent report.

Bankruptcy.

A legal concept that would be best to avoid. Also known as Insolvency, this occurs when an individual cannot meet their financial obligations within a reasonable time frame or if their liabilities exceed their assets.

Bid.

A method of purchasing real estate at auction by making an offer.

Borrowing.

When an individual business approaches a lender, such as a bank, to request a loan.

Capacity.

In financial terms, capacity is an individual's ability to repay a loan. When applying for financing, banks will look into factors such as income, job stability and other outstanding debts, including how much has been paid off. With a stable job and regular income, borrowers will often have a good lending capacity.

Cash.

Money, such as bills, coins and notes.

Caveat.

A property caveat is a claim to a property as a legal document. Creating a caveat allows both parties to claim their share of interest. Until the caveat is settled, no further transactions can be registered against the title.

Capital Gains Tax.

If you sell an asset such as investment property for a profit, you are subject to capital gains tax (CGT). At the end of the fiscal year, they add the capital gain to your income to be taxed.

Cheque.

Cheques detail any amount of money that is withdrawn by an account holder to make a payment. A cheque requires the account holder to write the total amount to pay in both written and numeric forms.

Court judgement.

If a person cannot repay their creditors, creditors can seek a judgement in court.

Commitment fee.

A fee is added onto a loan to compensate a lender for their commitment to offering to fund.

Contract of sale.

An agreement includes the terms and conditions signed, dated and witnessed by all related parties.

Conveyance.

When real estate is transferred from one party to another. In real estate, this could be when a seller transfers the ownership of a property to a buyer.

Collateral.

Collateral is protection to mitigate the risks involved with lending.

Credit.

While this refers to several aspects of lending, most used to describe a contract agreement where an individual receives money and repays the lender by a predetermined date (with an added interest fee).

Credit card.

You can use a plastic or metal card issued by a financial institution to borrow money up to a pre-approved limit.

The total you can take out will be decided by the financial institution that issues the card, and your credit history and score will also be considered.

Credit score.

Used by lenders to decide whether to accept funding applications based on the risk associated with the borrower. Also referred to as a credit rating.

Debt.

Debt is the amount of borrowed money that hasn't been paid back yet on loan. Mortgages, credit cards and bank loans are all common examples of debt finance.

Default.

If a person or institution responsible for repaying a loan or making an interest payment cannot meet that obligation on time, then they are in default.

Deposit.

The amount of money needed to be paid upfront as part of the loan agreement. The amount specified can often vary depending on a variety of circumstances.

Direct Debit.

When a direct debit is made, a statement shows the amount of money withdrawn and the name of the company that collected it.

Division of Property.

Fair distribution, or property division, divides property rights and obligations between divorced or De facto spouses and business partners.

Director.

An individual who manages a company's operations and can exercise the business' powers for whatever needs it may have.

Earnings.

The amount of money earned for doing a job. The amount of money you get from doing a job. It is derived from the verb *to earn*, which means getting something you have worked for.

Economy.

A summary of goods, services produced, distributed and sold within a region or country.

Equity.

Property equity is the difference between the remaining debt and the asset's capital value in question.

Exchange of Contracts.

When a seller purchases a signed a copy of the sale contract and then exchanges these documents, a binding agreement is created to document the sale of real estate on agreed terms. The parties are then bound to go ahead to settlement, subject to any cooling-off period that may apply.

Financial position.

An organisation's financial position refers to its assets, liabilities and equity balances. In a broader sense, the concept can describe the financial condition, which is determined by analysing and comparing its financial statements.

First mortgage.

When a borrower uses the property as security for the first time as collateral for a loan. If the mortgage repayments are not met as agreed, the lender can seize the security.

Glossary

Guarantor.

In property development transactions, lenders could need more security to reduce their risk should the developer default on a loan. This guarantee can take various forms, from cash to property.

Indicative offer.

Lenders often show or suggest that an offer may go ahead if conditions are met, also known as a conditional offer.

Initial Public Offering (IPO).

When a company raises capital from public investors by offering shares of a corporation in a public share issuance.

Insurance.

Insurance is a policy where the provider indemnifies against losses incurred in particular situations. The most common forms of insurance include vehicle, health, homeowner and health policies.

Interest rate.

The amount of interest charged on a loan, proportionate to the amount borrowed. Interest rates allow banks or lenders to profit when distributing funds.

Investment property.

A real estate purchase intends to earn rental income or capital gain.

Joint tenants.

Joint tenancy is the default type of shared ownership. There is no property division between the joint owners; each owns one hundred per cent of the property. Legal ownership of the property passes to the surviving joint owner when a joint owner dies.

Lawyer.

A lawyer is someone who practices law and deals with legal issues. A lawyer provides legal advice and represents people in court.

Lease agreements.

Lease agreements are made between the property owner and tenant to occupy real estate.

Legal fees.

Upon completion of a purchase, the solicitor or conveyancer will charge a fee for the legal work carried out during the purchase process. Solicitors charge a flat fee regardless of the property's value.

Letter of Offer.

When a lender issues a finance offer to a borrower, it can be accepted or rejected, depending on the borrower in question's acceptance.

Loan.

When you receive funding (whether from a bank or friend) with the promise of paying it back, often with the additional interest. The principal factor is how much is borrowed, and interest is how much extra you're charged for taking out the loan. Loans can either be secured or unsecured.

Loan to Value Ratio.

All lenders use a Loan to Value Ratio to assess risk when they consider funding and can have a tremendous impact on the terms offered. The term is often abbreviated to LTV (Loan to Values) or LVR (Loan to Value Ratio).

Litigation.

When disputes are resolved in court through litigation, unless the parties settle before trial, a judge may make the final decision for the parties in litigation.

Liabilities.

Liabilities are obligations between two parties that have not yet been completed or repaid.

Mortgage.

A debt passed onto a borrower from a lender secured by a property.

Mortgagee sale.

In the event of a default by the mortgagor, the mortgagee claims the security and resells to avoid economic losses.

Mortgagor.

A borrower (individual or company) has an interest in a property through a mortgage as security for credit advancement.

Non-conforming loans.

The term non-conforming loan refers to lending that does not meet the criteria for bank financing.

Overdrawn.

If an account holder spends more than is in their account, their balance will be a negative figure, e.g. £-20.00, but it will instead be shown as £20DR, indicating that the account is 20 pounds into its overdraft.

Passed in.

If the owner's reserve price has not been met, the property is not sold at auction; hence, it is passed in.

Payment.

This is any money that you've taken out of your account. This is also known as a withdrawal or debit.

Periodic lease.

Typical for residential properties, a periodic lease is permitted when a tenant continues to rent and occupy the property beyond the end of the lease agreement.

Principal and interest mortgage.

A standard mortgage, with the difference that repayments are part capital and part interest.

Private treaty sale.

The terms and conditions of a private sale between a seller and buyer to purchase the real estate vary from state to state.

Profit.

When the financial earnings of a business activity exceed the amount needed for the costs, taxes, etc. This could be when a company buys something and sells it for a higher price.

Property Maintenance.

Property owners will need to make decisions regarding building works and maintenance. The agent managing your property will manage and look after the property. This includes marketing your property, collecting rent and fixing any issues.

Property Settlement.

A legal process facilitated by the legal and financial representatives of the purchaser and the seller. Settlement occurs when ownership is passed from the seller to the buyer. The settlement date is determined in the contract of sale by the vendor.

Receipt.

A note issues to document any money that is deposited into your account. This is also known as *paid-in* or *credits*.

Rescind.

To stop a contract of sale.

Reserve Price.

The vendor agrees upon the minimum acceptable price before the auction.

Residential tenants.

In most cases, residential leases last for one year; any shorter would be costly for the property owner for re-tenanting costs such as marketing, rental income delays and re-letting fees to the agent.

Savings.

The amount of money you have left after obligations and personal expenditure is deducted from your total earnings. Savings are the amount of money you haven't spent on, for example, bills, restaurants or even risked investments.

Second mortgage.

A borrower can offer their real estate as collateral a second time to another lender while the first still has the finance secured. As a result, the next lender takes a second charge over the property.

Security.

Security on a mortgage is essential because it reduces the risk a lender takes when providing a loan. If a loan is backed by property, for example, then if the borrower defaults on repayments, the lender may seize the property to claim the outstanding debt.

Settlement Date.

The final part of the process whereby the purchaser completes the payment of the contract price to the seller, and legal possession is transferred to the purchaser.

Share certificates.

Whenever a company sells shares on the market, it issues shares certificates. As proof of ownership and as a record of the purchase, shares certificates are issued to shareholders.

Shareholders.

A person or business that owns a share in a company's stock. Shareholders can receive capital gains, take capital losses and may receive dividend payments. As equity owners, shareholders have the same benefits and drawbacks as Directors.

Share certificates.

A share certificate is a document that is issued by a company that sells shares. An investor receives a share certificate upon purchasing a certain number of shares and as a record of ownership.

Glossary

Spending.

Any form of paying out money. Similar words include *spend*, *disburse* and *squander*.

Standing order.

Regular, automated payment of the same amount from your account. Standing orders show how much was paid and who it went to.

Stamp duty.

Stamp duty arises from the sale or transfer of a wide range of personal and business assets.

Statement date.

A date showing when a statement was printed. Any transactions made after this date are put on the following statement.

Statement of Position.

Assets and liabilities, companies or individual positions show the current net equity position.

Tax.

Tax is a certain amount of money you have to pay the government out of your earnings. Taxes are used to fund education, healthcare, military, police and even construction projects.

Tax returns.

Tax authorities use this process to assess a taxpayer's liability based on their annual income, personal circumstances and any associated corporate entities.

Tenants in common.

A joint ownership arrangement exists when multiple individuals own the same property but neither has one hundred per cent ownership.

Trading.

A broad term for buying, selling or trading a commodity, whether wholesale or retail, within one country or between different ones, or even domestic or foreign trade. It can include business deals, transactions, an exchange of items, and more.

Valuer.

A company appointed to conduct the assessment of the current market value of the real estate.

Valuation.

Not to be confused with an appraisal, a valuation provides a more accurate and recognised property value.

Variation.

To change or alter the conditions of the contract of sale.

Vendor.

In a real estate transaction, a person (s) or entity sells the property.

Yield.

An indicator of income by percentage earned on real estate. It is calculated by the received net income and the market value of the real estate.

Zoning.

A form of local council planning that controls current and future developments, including residential, business, and industrial projects.

Follow us

This book is dedicated to all the children who haven't had the best start in life and need guidance on finances. For more information, check out our website or app to learn more. You can also follow us on Instagram, Facebook and YouTube. Keep up to date with our monthly updates to stay in touch and learn more about the complicated world of finance and how you can survive in it.

For further information about Sherwood Finance:

Call us 1800 743 796

head to the website
www.sherwoodfinance.com.au

follow us on Facebook, Instagram and Twitter.

www.ingramcontent.com/pod-product-compliance
Lightning Source LLC
Chambersburg PA
CBHW030302010526
44107CB00053B/1792